Ethel Price

The chest

Eggin and the Slinx are still tingling with the thrill of seeing the sunken ship.
Now they must get into it, and hunt for the riches.
They go down to the ship.
There is a big gash in the hull.
That's how they will get in.

Draw Eggin and the Slinx swimming down to the ship.
Write
Now the pals have to get into the ship.

Santa Monica

The two pals go scrambling into the hull, but then they come to a stop. They must not rush.
They can see that they are in a big cabin, but it is a mishmash of split planks and twisted metal.
The deck itself is just a mass of odds and ends.
They can see some pistols, muskets and cutlasses, buckets and pans, mugs and dishes, fragments of pots, cannon shot, and lots more.
The bits of the deck that they can see are rotten.
The ship is full of risks.
They must not trust it.

Draw the mess in the cabin.
Write
The ship is full of risks.

Eggin thinks they must get out of this cabin.
Eggin taps the Slinx on the back.
He signals to him with his hand.
The Slinx understands.
They creep out of the cabin, and swim up to the top deck.
They are in luck.
There is a hatch.
This will get them into the ship!

The two pals pull and tug at the hatch.
It is a difficult job, but at last they do it.
A set of steps goes down into the ship.
Eggin and the Slinx creep down.

Now they are in the depths of the ship.
They are going down a dim tunnel.
The deck is solid, but they still test every step.
They are ready for the unexpected.
They do not intend to get stuck.
At the end of the tunnel they can see a very grand cabin.
Will this cabin have all the riches?
They think it will!
Still testing every step, they travel down the tunnel.

Draw the tunnel with the cabin at the end.
Write
Eggin and the Slinx think that the riches are in this cabin.

Now Eggin and the Slinx are in the big cabin.
They can see the desk with a map and some instruments.
Next to the desk is a mat.
At the top of the cabin there is a grill, and suspended from the grill they can see a brass lamp.

Eggin goes across to one end of the cabin, where he can see a bunk.

What a shock!

Eggin jumps out of his skin.

There is a skeleton in the bunk.

Eggin panics.

He rushes across to the Slinx.

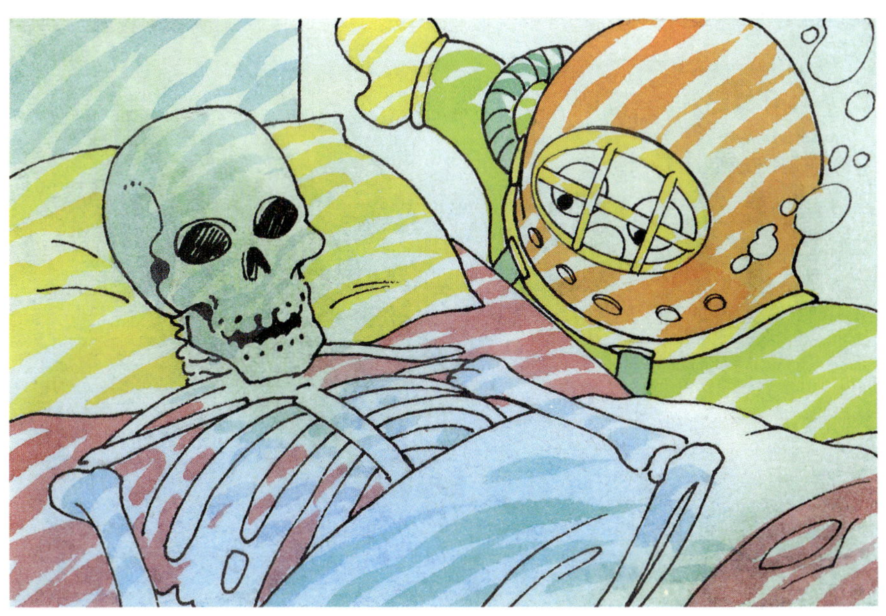

Draw the skeleton in the bunk.

Write

A skeleton gives Eggin a shock!

The Slinx has to hug and pat Eggin until at last he is ready to go back to the hunt.
They check the cabin from top to bottom, but they have run out of luck.
They cannot track down one bit of cash.
The Slinx gets mad.
He goes across to the desk and gives it a thump.
Then he kicks the mat.
The Slinx stops in his tracks.
Hidden under the mat, there is a hatch with a big metal ring!

Eggin and the Slinx rush to grab the ring.
They pull and pull, but it will not shift.
Then Eggin thinks of twisting the ring.
On the first twist, there is a dull click.
On the second twist, the hatch pops up!
There, in the bottom of the hatch, is a big chest.

The pals pull the chest out.
It is big and solid, with metal bands and a good lock.
The two pals get out of the cabin and up to the raft as fast as they can.
Then they tell the fuzzbuzzes that they have got to a big chest.
Now they must lift it out of the ship.
Everyone gets cracking.
The Slinx swims back down to the ship.
He swims across the top deck until he can see the grill.
Pushing and pulling, he shifts the grill.
Now he can swim down into the cabin.

He fixes some clips onto the chest, then he gives two tugs. Up on the raft everyone pulls.

The chest goes up.
Then, all of a sudden, it stops.
The Slinx cannot understand it.
He swims back up to the raft.
The fuzzbuzzes are flat out!
They tell him that they cannot pull the chest up.
'Pass down some plastic sacks!' yells the Slinx.
Now the fuzzbuzzes do not understand, but they give the sacks to the Slinx.
Grabbing them, he swims back down to the chest.
The Slinx pushes the sacks under the chest then he fills them with gas.
That does the trick.
The chest goes up and up!

Draw the chest going up.

Write

The gas in the sacks pulls the chest up.

Now the chest is on the raft.
The Slinx picks up a mallet and a chisel.

CRACK!

The lock drops onto the deck.
Now the band can lift the lid!
'Let the Slinx do it!' they all yell.
With a big grin, he does so.
It's astonishing!
The chest is full to the brim.
The band can see crosses and goblets, lockets and pendants, rings and medallions.
They have hit the jackpot!

Draw all the things in the chest.

Write

The band are rich at last.

The fuzzbuzzes do a little jig.
Eggin claps his hands.
The Slinx loves dressing up, so he puts on some of the stuff.
Everyone is happy.
They are rich at last.
But the band do not see what is happening out in the Atlantic.
They are in for it now!

Draw the Slinx with the things from the chest.

Write

Everyone is happy.
They do not see a bad spell coming.

The band are still giggling and chuckling as the tempest hits them.
First of all, the wind hits the raft full blast.
Within seconds, the sun is blotted out and it pelts down.
Then the Atlantic goes mad!
First it is rippling, then it is bubbling, then it is frothing, then it is a gushing, rushing torrent.
It hits, thumps and buffets them.
The panic-stricken fuzzbuzzes cling to the mast.
Eggin rushes across to help them.
The Slinx just stands there, he cannot understand it.

Write
A tempest hits the raft.
Draw this.

Eggin can see what is going to happen.
He yells out, but he cannot stop it.
The Atlantic hits them with a colossal, crushing thump, and the Slinx is swept off the raft.
Eggin can see him struggling in the cross-currents, but he can tell that the Slinx is going to go under.

Write
The Slinx is swept into the Atlantic.
Draw this.

Without thinking, Eggin dashes to the chest, tips it up, lifts it up, then sends it spinning across to the Slinx.
The Slinx grabs it with one hand, then Eggin and the fuzzbuzzes pull him back to the raft.

Write
Eggin acts fast.
He picks up the chest and sends it spinning across to the Slinx.
Now they can pull the Slinx back.
Draw this.

Then the wind drops and
the sun comes out.
The wet and unhappy band stand and inspect the chest.
All the riches have sunk to the bottom of the Atlantic.
The trinkets the Slinx put on have sunk as well.
There is nothing left.
Without a word, they travel back to land.

Write

All the riches have sunk to the bottom of the Atlantic.
There is nothing left.

The band tramps back up the rock steps to the top of the cliff. They flop down next to the cross. Eggin is very upset. He thinks he has lost the riches. 'Rubbish!' snaps the Slinx. And the fuzzbuzzes add, 'That chest kept the Slinx up, and it got him back to us. Thank you Eggin, you are the best of all pals!' They all grin. 'So we have lost the riches,' they yell. 'So what? The Slinx is fit and well. What good is millions in the bank if you do not have one pal? Forget the riches! We all love you!'

And with that, they all jump into the van and set off back.

1 Write down six things the pals see in the first cabin. (4)

2 Why do you think the pals test every step? (8)

3 Why does Eggin jump out of his skin? (11)

4 What is hidden under the mat? (12)

5 What do they have to do to get into the hidden hatch? (13)

6 On his second trip down, how does the Slinx get back into the cabin? (14)

7 How does the Slinx get the chest to go up? (16)

8 What happens to all the riches? (26)

9 In the end, the band forget the riches. Why? (30)